WHD

Provided

by

Measure B

which was approved

by the voters in

November, 1998

Hello, Family Members,

Learning to read is one of the most important accomplishments of early childhood. **Hello Reader!** books are designed to help children become skilled readers who like to read. Beginning readers learn to read by remembering frequently used words like "the," "is," and "and"; by using phonics skills to decode new words; and by interpreting picture and text clues. These books provide both the stories children enjoy and the structure they need to read fluently and independently. Here are suggestions for helping your child *before, during,* and *after* reading:

Before
- Look at the cover and pictures and have your child predict what the story is about.
- Read the story to your child.
- Encourage your child to chime in with familiar words and phrases.
- Echo read with your child by reading a line first and having your child read it after you do.

During
- Have your child think about a word he or she does not recognize right away. Provide hints such as "Let's see if we know the sounds" and "Have we read other words like this one?"
- Encourage your child to use phonics skills to sound out new words.
- Provide the word for your child when more assistance is needed so that he or she does not struggle and the experience of reading with you is a positive one.
- Encourage your child to have fun by reading with a lot of expression . . . like an actor!

After
- Have your child keep lists of interesting and favorite words.
- Encourage your child to read the books over and over again. Have him or her read to brothers, sisters, grandparents, and even teddy bears. Repeated readings develop confidence in young readers.
- Talk about the stories. Ask and answer questions. Share ideas about the funniest and most interesting characters and events in the stories.

I do hope that you and your child enjoy this book.

   —Francie Alexander
    Reading Specialist,
    Scholastic's Learning Ventures

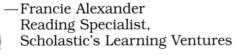

For my daughters, Greyson and Evanne,
and for Marion, the greatest Mom
—S.W.B.

To Chuckie Rowell,
recalling the day we all hung out with Mom
—G.F.

Text copyright © 2000 by Sonia W. Black.
Illustrations copyright © 2000 by George Ford.
All rights reserved. Published by Scholastic Inc.
SCHOLASTIC, HELLO READER, CARTWHEEL BOOKS
and associated logos are trademarks and/or
registered trademarks of Scholastic Inc.

Library of Congress Cataloging-in-Publication Data
Black, Sonia W.
    Hanging out with mom / by Sonia W. Black; illustrated by George Ford.
    p.   cm. — (Hello reader! Level 2)
    "Cartwheel books."
    Summary: After his mother gets home from work, a young boy enjoys spending the evening at the park with her.
    ISBN 0-590-86636-2
    [1. Mother and child–Fiction. 2. Parks–Fiction. 3. Stories in rhyme.]
    I. Ford, George Cephas, ill. II. Title. III. Series.

PZ8.3.B5715Han 1997

[E]–dc20

96–21308
CIP
AC

12 11 10 9 8 7 6 5   01 02 03 04

Printed in the U.S.A.   24
First Printing, April 2000

Hanging Out with Mom

by Sonia W. Black
Illustrated by George Ford

Hello Reader! — Level 2

SCHOLASTIC INC.

New York Toronto London Auckland Sydney
Mexico City New Delhi Hong Kong

Mommy is home!
Hooray! Hooray!
"Did you have fun at work?" I say.
"Can we go to the park to play?"

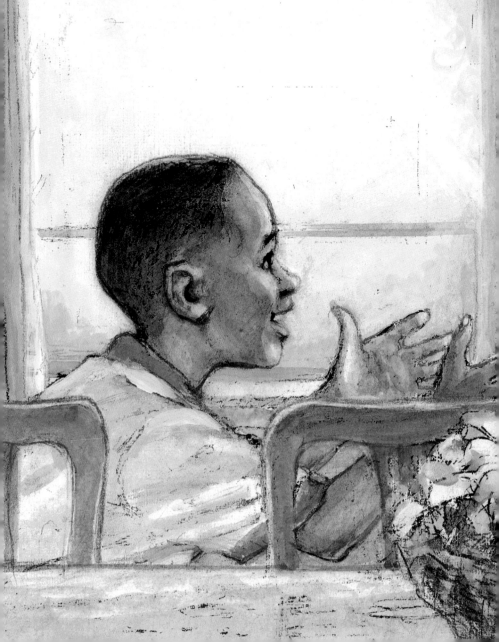

Mommy kicks off her shoes.
She says, "Okay!"

She changes her clothes.
We're on our way!

First we stop for a little snack.
Dinner can wait till we get back.

The park is full of runners and hikers

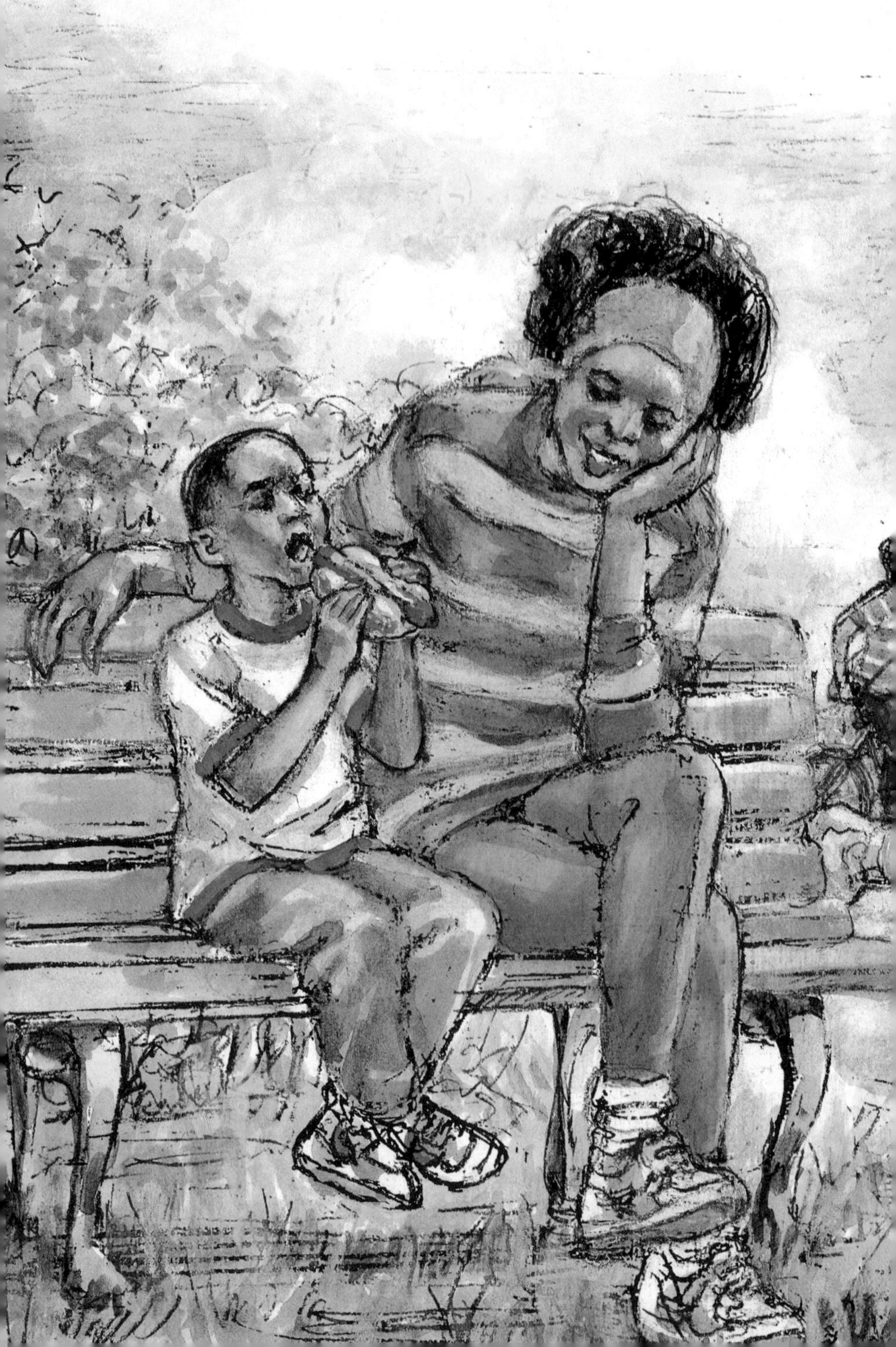

basketball players
and skaters and bikers.

Look! A rabbit! Look! There are two
They play leapfrog as people do!

The big kids fly kites high in the sky.
I chase their tails as they sail by.

Ducks swim slowly in a row.
They come to eat the crumbs we throw.

We see the playground. We run there fas

I am first. Mommy is last.

I go down the slide. One! Two! Three!
Mommy waits at the bottom for me.

Up to the top,
I climb and climb.
"Be careful," says Mommy.
"Please, take your time."

Sand! Sand!
It's everywhere!
There is sand in our shoes.
We have sand in our hair.

We have so much fun.
We haven't a care.

All too soon, it's getting dark.
It's time to go. We leave the park

But we will come back again to play,
because this is the best time of our day.